Don't let Fear Win

Catharine LJ Parks

Published by Catharine LJ Parks, 2024.

DON'T LET FEAR WIN

First edition. April 18, 2024.

Copyright © 2024 Catharine LJ Parks.

ISBN: 979-8227230157

Written by Catharine LJ Parks.

Also by Catharine LJ Parks

Obese People
Obesity Strongholds: How to Overcome Them

Standalone
The Ins and Outs of Gastric Bypass
Tips For Successful Dining Out
I am a Keto Kid
Why Remain Morbidly Obese
Ten Fads to Stay Clear of
Don't let Fear Win
Arguing With God

Watch for more at www.catharineljparks.com.

Table of Contents

CHAPTER 1
INTRODUCTION

Fear is a powerful force that resides within us. It lurks in the shadows, ready to pounce when we least expect it. It affects our thoughts, behaviours, and decisions, holding us back from reaching our full potential.

However, fear is conquerable. It's about stepping into the light beyond fear and reclaiming our power to live courageously, resiliently, and fulfilled.

This book aims to unmask Fear, exploring its roots, manifestations, and the multifaceted approaches necessary to overcome it. This book serves as a guide to understanding, embracing, and ultimately transcending fear.

Ever since humanity fell in the Garden of Eden, we have all been born into a sinful nature. We are all subject to fear, our enemy's greatest weapon.

This book offers simple solutions to battling fears. We are not alone in this universe.

Our enemy constantly battles our souls to keep us from having a successful relationship with our Creator and fulfilling our life purpose. But God's Word, the Holy Scriptures, gives us words of life that will encourage and inspire us to do what God has sent each of us here to do.

This book is informative, encouraging, and inspirational. It provides insights from God's Word on how to overcome fear and its effects.

The book also offers helpful suggestions to assist readers in conquering their fears and finding peace, joy, and love.

Readers will confidently learn to trust God's promises by exploring biblical principles and practical applications.

We are to do everything for God's glory, regardless of our position or where life takes us. God's Word tells us in 1 John 4:18: "There is no fear in love, but perfect love casteth out fear **because** fear has torment. He that feareth is not made perfect in love."

This profound truth underscores the transformative power of divine love. It teaches us that love and fear cannot coexist. Perfect love eliminates fear because fear brings pain and suffering. The one who fears cannot experience God's perfect love.

How can we attain ideal love? Is it possible to live without fear? As we draw closer to God, our fear diminishes, and we experience His perfect love.

This book will guide you on a journey of spiritual growth, helping you cultivate a deeper relationship with God, where fear has no place.

Through reflection, prayer, and applying biblical wisdom, you will discover the peace that surpasses all understanding and the courage to live boldly in the face of fear.

The following chapters will explore practical steps and spiritual disciplines that empower us to confront and overcome fear.

We will examine stories of faith from the Bible, learn from the experiences of others who have triumphed over their fears and engage in exercises designed to strengthen our faith and Resilience.

By the end of this journey, you will be equipped with the knowledge and faith needed to live a life free from the chains of fear, fully embracing the purpose and destiny that God has ordained for you.

Join us in this transformative journey. Let us together learn how to conquer fear, live in the light of God's love, and fulfill our divine purpose with courage and unwavering faith.

CHAPTER 2

WHAT IS FEAR?

Fear can be a powerful motivator that drives us to overcome obstacles and achieve great things. It is a natural response to the challenges we face. It can help us reach our full potential when harnessed with determination and Resilience.

Fear is an adaptive response that evolved to help organisms survive in dangerous situations by triggering a "fight-or-flight" reaction.

When we encounter something scary, our bodies undergo physiological changes such as increased heart rate, rapid breathing, heightened alertness, and muscle tension. These changes prepare us to confront or flee the threat.

Historical Origins of Fear

Our ancestors relied on fear to stay alive in dangerous environments. This primal instinct helped them avoid predators and other threats, ensuring the species' survival.

Today, though our environments have drastically changed, the fear response remains deeply embedded in our biology.

Fear can be triggered by various stimuli, including physical danger, social situations, uncertainty, failure, loss, or trauma.

The intensity of fear can range from mild apprehension to intense terror. It can manifest in various ways, such as phobias, anxiety disorders, or panic attacks.

Delving Deeper into Fear

1. **Physiological Response**

Fear initiates a series of automatic responses in the body. These include the release of adrenaline and cortisol, which prepare the body to confront or escape the threat.

This response, known as the "fight-or-flight" mechanism, is essential for survival. It enables a rapid reaction to danger, increasing our chances of safety.

2. **Psychological Impact**:

Fear can profoundly impact our mental state. It can lead to heightened awareness and focus, which can be beneficial in dangerous situations.

However, chronic fear or anxiety can be debilitating, leading to stress, depression, and a diminished quality of life.

Understanding how to manage and mitigate these effects is crucial for maintaining mental health.

3. **Behavioral Reactions**:

Fear influences our behaviour in significant ways. It can drive us to take protective actions, seek safety, or avoid risky situations.

While these behaviours can be adaptive, excessive fear can lead to avoidance patterns that limit our experiences and hinder personal growth.

4. **Types of Fear**:

Fear can be categorized into several types based on its source and manifestation. Common types include:

Phobias

Intense, irrational fears of specific objects or situations, such as heights (acrophobia) or spiders (arachnophobia).

Anxiety Disorders

Anxiety Disorders consist of persistent and excessive worry that can interfere with daily activities. These are generalized anxiety disorder (GAD) or social anxiety disorder (SAD).

Panic Attacks

Sudden episodes of intense fear and physical symptoms often occur without an obvious trigger.

Existential Dread

DON'T LET FEAR WIN

A profound sense of unease or fear related to the fundamental aspects of human existence. It encompasses deep philosophical concerns about life, death, freedom, meaning, and the nature of the self.

Key Aspects of Existential Dread

1. **Fear of Meaninglessness**

Description

This involves the anxiety that life might be inherently meaningless or devoid of purpose.

Example

A person may feel overwhelmed by the notion that their efforts, achievements, and existence may ultimately have no lasting significance.

2. **Awareness of Mortality**

Description

This is the anxiety stemming from recognizing one's mortality and the inevitability of death.

Example

Realizing that one's life is finite can lead to existential dread, provoking thoughts about what happens after death and whether anything endures.

3. **Isolation**

Description

This refers to the feeling of being fundamentally alone in the universe.

Example

Even in the presence of others, an individual may feel a deep sense of isolation, as though no one else can fully understand their unique experience.

4. **Freedom and Responsibility**

Description

The realization that we have complete freedom to make choices, coupled with the responsibility for the consequences, can be a source of dread.

Example

The burden of creating one's path in life, possibly making wrong or harmful decisions, can be daunting.

5. **Absurdity**

Description

This is the recognition of the absurd or irrational nature of human existence.

Example

The struggle to find order or reason in a chaotic and indifferent universe can lead to feelings of absurdity and futility.

Examples in Literature and Philosophy

Jean-Paul Sartre

A prominent existentialist philosopher who explored themes of existential dread, particularly in his work "Being and Nothingness."

Sartre discussed the idea of "nausea" as a response to the realization of the absurdity and contingency of existence.

Albert Camus

In "The Myth of Sisyphus," Camus describes the human condition as fundamentally absurd and suggests that we must find meaning despite this absurdity.

The constant struggle against meaninglessness can lead to existential dread.

Coping with Existential Dread

1. **Acceptance and Embracing Absurdity**

Accepting the absurdity of life and finding personal meaning despite it can be a way to cope.

This perspective encourages living authentically and fully engaging with life.

1. **Engagement in Meaningful Activities**

Finding purpose in activities, relationships, and passions can provide a sense of meaning and counteract feelings of dread.

1. **Existential Therapy**

This therapy focuses on helping individuals confront and embrace their existential concerns, fostering a deeper understanding of themselves and their place in the world.

1. **Mindfulness and Meditation**

Practices encouraging living in the present moment can help alleviate anxiety about the future and the unknown.

Existential dread is a profound and deeply human experience rooted in our awareness of life's most fundamental questions and uncertainties.

While it can be unsettling, it also offers an opportunity for deep reflection and personal growth.

By acknowledging and exploring these existential concerns, individuals can find ways to live more authentically and meaningfully, even in inherent uncertainties.

Fear vs. Anxiety

While fear and anxiety are related, they differ in their nature and intensity. Fear is a response to an immediate threat, while anxiety is a generalized feeling of unease about potential future threats.

Understanding this distinction helps in addressing each condition appropriately.

Coping Mechanisms

There are various strategies to cope with and manage fear, including:

Mindfulness and Relaxation Techniques

Practices such as meditation, deep breathing, and progressive muscle relaxation can help reduce the physical symptoms of fear.

Cognitive Behavioral Therapy (CBT)

A type of psychotherapy that helps individuals identify and change negative thought patterns that contribute to fear and anxiety.

Exposure Therapy

Gradually exposing oneself to the feared object or situation in a controlled manner to reduce sensitivity and fear over time.

Support Systems

Leaning on friends, family, or support groups can provide comfort and perspective, helping to mitigate fear.

Understanding fear in its entirety allows us to address it effectively. By exploring physiological, psychological, and behavioural aspects, we can develop strategies to manage and overcome fear.

This book provides the insights and tools needed to transform fear from a paralyzing force into a powerful motivator for personal growth and achievement.

CHAPTER 3

UNDERSTANDING FEAR

Fear is a natural response to perceived threats, triggering physiological changes and emotional reactions.

While necessary for human survival, excessive or irrational fear can become problematic, leading to avoidance behaviours and interfering with daily functioning. Understanding and managing fear is crucial for emotional regulation and personal growth.

Anxiety

Anxiety describes feelings of unease, worry, or nervousness about uncertain future events.

It often involves anticipating these events and can manifest through physical symptoms such as increased heart rate, sweating, trembling, and difficulty concentrating.

Anxiety can range from mild to severe and may be a normal reaction to stress or a symptom of mental health disorders, such as generalized anxiety disorder (GAD), panic disorder, or social anxiety disorder.

Worrying

Worrying is closely related to anxiety and can be considered a form of fear, albeit more generalized and focused on potential future events or outcomes.

While fear typically responds to an immediate threat, worrying often involves apprehension or concern about various aspects of life, such as work, relationships, health, or finances.

Key points about worrying include:

Future-oriented

Involves thoughts and concerns about future events, possibilities, or outcomes, often revolving around "what-if" scenarios.

Negative anticipation

Involves anticipating adverse outcomes or consequences, imagining worst-case scenarios, and dwelling on potential problems.

Physical and emotional symptoms

It can include difficulty concentrating on sleeping, gastrointestinal issues, irritability, and feeling on edge.

Impact on functioning

Excessive worrying can interfere with daily life, leading to avoidance of certain situations or activities, difficulty making decisions, and impaired social or occupational functioning.

While worrying is similar to fear and anxiety, it differs in focus and intensity. Fear is typically more immediate and focused on a specific threat.

At the same time, worrying is more generalized and focused on potential future concerns. However, worrying can escalate into anxiety if it becomes persistent, excessive, and distressing.

Panic Attacks

A panic attack is a sudden episode of intense fear or discomfort that peaks within minutes and is accompanied by various physical and cognitive symptoms, including:

Rapid heartbeat or palpitations

Sweating

Trembling or shaking

Shortness of breath or a feeling of choking

Chest pain or discomfort

Nausea or abdominal distress

Dizziness or light-headedness

Feelings of derealization or depersonalization (feeling detached from oneself or reality)

Fear of losing control or going crazy

Fear of dying

Numbness or tingling sensations

Chills or hot flashes

Panic attacks can be spontaneous and unpredictable, often without an apparent trigger. They can also occur in specific situations or environments, particularly those associated with previous panic attacks or intense fear.

Understanding fear, anxiety, worrying, and panic attacks is crucial for managing these emotions effectively.

By recognizing their characteristics and effects, individuals can develop strategies to cope with and reduce the impact of these experiences on their lives.

CHAPTER 4

UNMASKING FEAR

Fear is a primal emotion ingrained in the fabric of human existence, with tendrils that reach back through the annals of history and weave through the complex tapestry of psychology.

Its influence extends beyond mere emotional reactions; it permeates our behaviours, dictates our decision-making processes, and profoundly impacts our overall well-being.

From the irrational dread triggered by phobias to the pervasive unease of anxiety disorders, from the haunting spectre of past traumas to the existential dread of confronting life's uncertainties.

Fear manifests in myriad forms, each exerting its grip on the human psyche in distinct ways.

Effectively grappling with fear requires a multifaceted approach. First and foremost is recognizing its triggers—the catalysts that ignite the flames of apprehension within us. These triggers can be as diverse as the individuals themselves, ranging from specific objects or situations to abstract concepts that tap into our most profound insecurities. By identifying these triggers, we can unravel the tangled web of fear and gain insight into its origins.

Going deeper into the subject, understanding the underlying causes of fear reveals a complex interplay of biology, psychology, and personal experiences that give rise to its existence. According to evolutionary psychologists, fear evolved as a protective mechanism to safeguard our ancestors from immediate threats in their hostile environments.

This primal instinct persists, though often in contexts far removed from our ancestors' savannahs.

In addition, psychological theories emphasize the role of conditioning, upbringing, and societal influences in shaping our fear responses. This highlights the intricate interplay of nature and nurture in shaping our emotional landscape.

Yet, understanding fear is only the first step; the true challenge lies in dismantling its hold on our lives. This necessitates cultivating effective coping strategies—tools and techniques that empower us to confront our fears head-on and reclaim agency over our emotional well-being.

Various strategies may be used to help individuals overcome their fears and anxieties. These strategies may include cognitive-behavioural techniques to change negative thought patterns and exposure therapy to help individuals become less sensitive to their fears. Mindfulness practices to build resiliency and therapeutic interventions to address past traumas and promote healing.

The journey toward overcoming fear is a deeply personal odyssey that demands introspection, resilience, and a willingness to confront the shadows lurking within our minds.

By shedding light on our fears' darkness, we pave the way toward a future characterized not by paralysis and apprehension but by courage, resilience, and profound self-awareness.

CHAPTER 5

THE PARALYSIS OF FEAR

Fear can be overwhelming, stunting personal growth and eroding one's sense of well-being, leading to fear-induced paralysis. This can result in avoidance being the primary response to challenges or opportunities for growth, preferring the false safety of familiar surroundings. Perfectionism can also be born from the fear of failure or judgment, leading individuals to pursue unattainable standards and perpetuating a cycle of dissatisfaction and self-criticism. Self-doubt, amplified by fear, casts a shadow over one's abilities and potential, undermining confidence and thwarting aspirations.

Breaking free from fear's suffocating embrace requires a courageous commitment to counteract its insidious influence. Embracing imperfection and vulnerability is a revolutionary act that challenges the illusion of flawlessness and celebrates the beauty inherent in authenticity. By acknowledging that growth is messy and nonlinear, individuals liberate themselves from the suffocating grip of perfectionism and open themselves to the rich tapestry of human experience, feeling empowered and free.

Challenging negative beliefs is another pivotal step to liberation from fear's grip. By questioning the validity of distorted thoughts and reframing them with compassionate understanding, individuals reclaim agency over their inner narrative and cultivate a mindset rooted in resilience and self-empowerment. This process requires courage and persistence, but the rewards are profound—a newfound sense of clarity, confidence, and self-worth that serves as a sturdy foundation for personal growth.

Taking small steps is a powerful antidote to fear-induced paralysis. By breaking daunting tasks or goals into manageable increments, individuals mitigate overwhelm and cultivate a sense of momentum and progress. Each small victory serves as a beacon of hope, illuminating the path forward and bolstering confidence in one's ability to navigate challenges and overcome obstacles.

Practicing self-compassion is a balm and a lifeline for the wounds inflicted by fear. In moments of vulnerability and self-doubt, extending kindness and understanding to oneself fosters resilience. It fortifies the spirit against the onslaught of fear's assaults. Through self-compassion, individuals cultivate a nurturing inner dialogue, replacing self-criticism with self-acceptance and fostering a sense of inner peace and tranquillity. This practice is not just a tool but a testament to your strength and resilience, offering you the support and understanding you need in your journey to overcome fear-induced paralysis.

Seeking support is a courageous act of vulnerability that can catalyze profound transformation. Whether through the guidance of trusted friends, mentors, or mental health professionals, reaching out for support creates a network of safety and validation, reminding individuals that they are not alone in their struggles. In the compassionate embrace of community, individuals find solace, encouragement, and the strength to confront fear head-on, knowing they are supported every step.

Overcoming fear's grip is a journey of profound self-discovery and empowerment. It requires courage, resilience, and a steadfast commitment to growth. By embracing imperfection, challenging negative beliefs, taking small steps, practicing self-compassion, and seeking support, individuals can transcend fear-induced paralysis and unlock their boundless potential.

CHAPTER 6

FEAR IS A SPIRIT

In the Bible, fear is depicted as a spiritual force or presence that can influence people's thoughts, actions, and faith.

Fear is a "spirit from the dark side" sent to control, take over, and manipulate human minds. The fruit of its completion is to bring about a pervasive and evil presence in our lives.

This is how fear operates in humanity. Here, you will find just how fear operates to stop our spiritual growth.

Invisibility and Intangibility

Fear is a spirit that possesses the eerie ability to operate in the hidden recesses of our minds, evading detection by our conscious awareness.

It dwells in the shadows of our consciousness, subtly influencing our thoughts, emotions, and behaviours without us even realizing it.

It murmurs its insidious messages, planting seeds of doubt, worry, and apprehension within us.

At times, fear remains elusive, its presence masked by the distractions of daily life or buried beneath layers of denial.

Yet, despite its stealthy nature, its impact is anything but subtle.

Its tendrils reach deep into our souls, shaping our perceptions, distorting our beliefs, and dictating our actions in ways we may not fully comprehend.

Fear's influence extends far beyond the confines of our individual minds, permeating our relationships, communities, and even society as a whole. It breeds distrust, division, and conflict, sowing discord and chaos wherever it takes hold.

Though we may strive to ignore or suppress it, fear's effects are undeniable, manifesting in anxiety, stress, and a pervasive sense of unease. It casts a shadow over our aspirations, stifling our dreams and imprisoning us in a cycle of self-doubt and limitation.

Yet, despite its formidable presence, fear is not invincible. By shining the light of awareness into the darkness of our consciousness, we can begin to unravel its hold on us.

Spiritually, we can shine our light into our darkness and call on the Lord to fight those tendrils of fear.

We must step out in faith and ask the Lord to give us courage and compassion while looking inward to gain introspection into the source of our fear. Then, we can confront our fears head-on and forge a path toward freedom and authenticity.

Malevolence and Manipulation**

Fear operates subtly, like a cunning whisperer in our minds. It doesn't just scare us; it distorts reality, making us believe lies about ourselves and the world.

It preys on our weaknesses and magnifies them until we're frozen in place, unable to act.

Imagine fear as a deceptive voice constantly whispering falsehoods and exaggerations, creating a distorted version of reality.

It targets our vulnerabilities, amplifying them until they overshadow everything else.

This distortion can cloud our judgment, making us see dangers where there are none and preventing us from taking necessary risks or pursuing our goals.

Contagious Influence

Because it is a dark spirit, fear has a contagious nature. It can spread from person to person, infecting entire communities or societies with its toxic energy.

Fearmongers exploit this, using fear to control and manipulate others.

Feeding on Negativity

Fear has a symbiotic relationship with negative emotions such as doubt, anxiety, and despair. Here's how it flourishes within them:

Doubt

When we doubt ourselves or our abilities, fear capitalizes on this uncertainty. It whispers insidious thoughts, amplifying our insecurities and casting doubt on our potential for success or happiness.

This self-doubt feeds the fear, making it more substantial and more pervasive.

Anxiety

Anxiety is like fertile ground for fear to take root. It thrives on the constant worry and apprehension that anxiety brings.

Fear latches onto the "what-ifs" and worst-case scenarios, heightening our sense of unease and perpetuating a cycle of fear and anxiety.

Despair

In moments of despair, when we feel hopeless or overwhelmed by life's challenges, fear finds ample opportunity to flourish.

It convinces us that things will never improve and that we are doomed to failure or suffering.

This sense of despair feeds into the fear, reinforcing its grip on our souls.

Fear uses these negative emotions as fuel, feeding off them to sustain its power over us. It distorts our perceptions, magnifying our fears and making them seem impossible. As a result, we become trapped in a cycle of negativity, with fear at the center, draining our energy and undermining our confidence.

Breaking free from this cycle requires confronting our fears and challenging the negative thoughts and emotions that fuel them. By cultivating self-awareness, practicing self-compassion, and seeking support when needed, we can weaken fear's hold and reclaim control over our lives.

Illusions of Power

Fear can sometimes trick us into thinking it's our protector, masquerading as strength. It convinces us by giving in to its demands—like avoiding risks, sticking to familiar things, or reacting aggressively—. But this false sense of security only traps us even more.

Resistance and Rebellion

Certainly, overcoming fear is not a one-time battle but a continuous journey. It requires perseverance and Resilience in the face of adversity. We may stumble and fall along the way, but each setback is an opportunity to learn and grow stronger. By facing our fears head-on, we liberate ourselves from their grip and inspire others to do the same.

Together, we can create a ripple effect of courage and empowerment, transforming the darkness of fear into the brightness of possibility and freedom.

Transformation and Redemption

Confronting our fears isn't just about overcoming obstacles but reclaiming our true selves. As we challenge the lies and distortions fear imposes upon us, we embark on a profound transformation and redemption journey. By shedding the shackles of fear, we unlock our potential and embrace authenticity. This liberation allows us to live fully and authentically, no longer bound by fear's oppressive influence. In doing so, we transform our lives and inspire others to break free from the chains of fear and step into their own power.

Eternal Vigilance

The battle against fear is ongoing, and we must guard against this persistent dark spirit. It demands continuous vigilance and self-awareness to prevent its insidious influence from creeping back into our lives.

Yet, with mindfulness as our shield and resilience as our sword, we can fortify ourselves against fear's advances.

Moreover, the support of others acts as a beacon of light in our darkest moments, guiding us toward courage and truth.

Together, we can stand firm against fear's onslaught, embracing the radiant light of courage and authenticity.

1. **2 Timothy 1:7 (NIV)**states: "For the Spirit God gave us does not make us timid, but gives us power, love, and self-discipline.

The following verses discuss the concept of fear in a spiritual context. They tell us that fear is not from God's spirit and works against His power, love, and self-discipline.

In **1 John 4:18 (NIV)**, fear is described as incompatible with love, and perfect love drives it out.

Psalm 23:4 (NIV) associates fear with evil and darkness while highlighting God's presence as a source of comfort and protection. These verses convey that fear is a spiritual force that opposes God and His love and should not be embraced or accepted.

Isaiah 41:10 (NIV) states, "So do not fear, for I am with you; do not be dismayed, for I am your God. I will strengthen, help, and uphold you with my righteous right hand."

This verse reassures believers not to fear because God is with them.

Fear is presented as something that can be overcome through God's presence and strength, indicating its spiritual nature as an opposing force to God's promises of protection and support.

These examples from the Bible illustrate fear as a spiritual concept that opposes God's spirit of power, love, and comfort.

They emphasize the importance of trust and faith in God to overcome fear.

CHAPTER 7

OVERCOMING FEAR
CASE STUDIES

Case studies illustrate how faith, prayer, and Divine Intervention can overcome fear in various contexts, such as fear of rejection and forgiveness. Each case highlights the transformative power of confronting fear and embracing courage.

These chapters provide a comprehensive understanding of fear and practical strategies for overcoming it. They emphasize the importance of faith, self-compassion, and seeking support.

Case Study #1

I used to be terrified of singing in church, fearing everyone would stare at me if I sang. The enemy of my soul exploited my loud voice to amplify this fear, creating an intense inner struggle that persisted until I decided to confront it. Determined to sing for the Lord, I boldly declared to the enemy that I would use it for Him since God gave me this voice. This declaration shattered the struggle, and I have been singing fearlessly since then. I have even recorded music and performed for special events.

Although I have conquered my fear of singing in public, I still battle anxiety induced by my spiritual enemy.

Whenever I face moments of performing or recording, I turn to prayer for strength.

Yet, I firmly believe the Lord is by my side, assisting me each time I call upon Him.

I have witnessed firsthand the transformative power of Jesus' name and trust that it will continue to help me overcome my fears.

A few years ago, I envisioned myself confidently singing in front of a large crowd. This dream remains close to my heart, and I am sure it will manifest someday. I eagerly anticipate the moment when I will stand victorious before an audience and fulfill the purpose God has ordained for me.

Philippians 4:13 (AMP)

I can do all things [which He has called me to do] through Him who strengthens and empowers me [to fulfill His purpose—I am self-sufficient in Christ's sufficiency; I am ready for anything and equal to anything through Him who infuses me with inner strength and confident peace.]

Case Study # 2

A few years ago, I was at odds with a family member, a disagreement that stirred deep distress within me. Despite the foundational principle of forgiveness in my Christian faith, I struggled to release the hurt and betrayal I felt. Painful memories and haunting flashbacks made it challenging to move forward.

The adversary sought to exploit this vulnerability, whispering insidious lies that forgiveness would only lead to further rejection and disrespect. Succumbing to pride and fear, I hesitated to confront the issue, fearing the worst possible outcome.

The enemy found satisfaction in our silence and reluctance to extend forgiveness. Yet, as followers of Christ, we are called to a higher standard. Though daunting, forgiveness is not an option to evade. It is the path to liberation from fear and pain.

Recognizing my inability to forgive alone, I prayed, seeking divine Intervention.

Through sincere supplication, I experienced the fulfillment of God's promise to aid us in forgiveness.

In a pivotal moment, I encountered the individual once more, testing the depths of my forgiveness. To my immense relief, I found no traces of bitterness or resentment within me. It was a profound victory—a testament to the transformative power of divine assistance.

This journey reaffirmed my belief that, with God's guidance, forgiveness is attainable for anyone, regardless of the magnitude of hurt or betrayal.

Case Study #3

A few years back, I had the profound opportunity to connect with my biological family, including my youngest sister. In our initial encounters, she exhibited signs of fear toward people. At merely five years old, she was unfamiliar with me, having only been informed of my existence as her sister. Despite this, she remained reticent, taking considerable time before opening up.

As I delved deeper into our relationship, I uncovered the shadows of past trauma that had cast a pall over her emotional growth. It was revealed that in her formative years, she had been a witness to the abuse suffered by her siblings. Recognizing the gravity of her struggles, I resolved to extend patience, empathy, and unwavering support to aid her in overcoming her fear of people.

Over time, I invested more in nurturing our bond, patiently guiding her toward trust and security. Through countless moments of understanding and affection, she gradually began to thaw, finding solace in the assurance of my steadfast presence.

It was a journey fraught with challenges and emotional hurdles, yet our profound connection made every trial worthwhile. Today, my sister is a testament to resilience, embodying a quiet strength tempered by her lingering shyness.

I cherish the privilege of having her as my sibling. However, for those grappling with trust and the fear of people, the journey towards healing often necessitates divine Intervention.

In seeking God's grace, we relinquish our fears and embrace His boundless love and peace to mend our wounded spirits.

We must heed the wisdom of Psalm 146:3 (AMP), which admonishes us not to place our trust in mortal beings devoid of salvation:

"Put not your trust in princes nor the son of man without salvation."

It is crucial to recognize that feeling afraid does not render us cowardly; instead, our response to fear defines our character.

Succumbing to fear relinquishes our agency, rendering us stagnant and unproductive.

Thus, we must fortify our spirits against fear's debilitating grasp, allowing Courage and faith to guide our steps toward growth and fulfillment.

CHAPTER 8

EMBRACING FEAR

Embracing fear involves acknowledging and accepting your fears instead of ignoring or suppressing them.

It means facing your fears head-on, understanding their origins, and using them as opportunities for growth.

Rather than letting fear control you, embracing it allows you to harness its energy to propel yourself forward.

It's about befriending your fears instead of letting them hold you back.

Acknowledging Fear

Acknowledging fear means recognizing and accepting that you are feeling afraid. It involves being honest with yourself about your emotions and understanding their reasons.

When you acknowledge your fear, you don't dismiss or ignore it; instead, you give it space to exist without judgment.

This step is crucial as it lays the foundation for effectively dealing with fear and progressing despite it.

Understanding Fear

Understanding fear involves uncovering the root causes behind it. This means identifying the underlying reasons or triggers. Fear can often be linked to past experiences, beliefs, or insecurities.

Examining these factors gives you insight into why you react the way you do. Once the cause is identified, you're better equipped to address it and overcome the fear.

Normalizing Fear

Normalizing fear means recognizing that it is a natural and shared human experience. Everyone feels afraid sometimes, and it's nothing to be ashamed of.

By normalizing fear, you acknowledge it as a normal part of life, not a sign of weakness.

Just as everyone gets hungry or tired, everyone feels afraid at times. Accepting this helps people face challenges with a healthier mindset.

Focus on Self-Compassion

When dealing with fear, practice self-compassion. Treat yourself as you would a friend going through a tough time—with kindness and care.

Understand that fear is normal and does not diminish your worth. You deserve love and acceptance, no matter what you're afraid of. Be gentle with yourself as you face your fears.

Reframing Fear as Opportunities

Reframe fear as a chance to grow rather than a roadblock. Fear often appears when stepping out of your comfort zone or facing challenges. Use it as a springboard for progress instead of letting it hold you back.

By seeing fear as a sign that you're stretching yourself and seizing new opportunities, you can turn its power into fuel for your journey.

Shift your perspective from worrying about what could go wrong to focusing on what you might gain or learn from the experience.

Think of fear as a cousin of excitement. Both stir your body with adrenaline, making you feel jittery and alert.

Instead of letting fear paralyze you, transform it into excitement. This mindset shift allows you to use fear's energy to propel yourself.

CHAPTER 9

BIBLICAL ASSURANCES TO CONQUER FEAR

ISAIAH 54: 14 (AMP)

You will establish yourself in righteousness (rightness, in conformity with God's will and order). You will be far from oppression or destruction, for you will not fear, and from terror, for it will not come near you.

Living a righteous life guarantees God's protection and removes fear.

ISAIAH 41: 10 (AMP)

Fear not (there is nothing to fear), for I am with you; do not look around you in terror and be dismayed, for I am your God. I will strengthen and harden you to difficulties; I will help you; I will hold you up and retain you with My (victorious) right hand of rightness and justice. (Acts 18:10.)

What an incredible promise from our Father!

Hebrews 13:5,6 (AMP)

Let your character [your moral essence, your inner nature] be free from the love of money [shun greed—be financially ethical], being content with what you have, for He has said, "I will never [under any circumstances] desert you [nor give you up nor leave you without support, nor will I in any degree leave you helpless], nor will I forsake or let you down or relax My hold on you [assuredly not]!"

So, we are comforted and encouraged and confidently say, "The Lord is my helper [in time of need]; I will not be afraid. What will man do to me?"

Trusting and relying on God, who loves us unconditionally, is crucial. During adversity, we can remind Him of His promises, and He will deliver us from all fears.

1 Samuel 12:24

"We should fear and serve the Lord with all our hearts, living in truth and acknowledging all He has done for us. Our motives and intentions are known to God, and He desires that we approach Him with reverence and respect.

It is not His intention for us to be afraid of Him but to serve Him willingly and out of love. He gave us free will to choose whether we want to serve Him.

However, it is essential to remember that we are His children, and He loves us dearly.

God promises to be with us every step of the way, in every situation or crisis, and He will never leave or forsake us."

Psalm 27:1

The Lord is my light and salvation; whom shall I fear? The Lord is the strength of my life; of whom shall I be afraid?

When we invite Jesus into our hearts, He becomes the guiding light that illuminates our path. The gift of salvation grants us the privilege of becoming heirs to Jesus Christ.

Salvation is not solely about accepting the Lord into our lives and hearts.

Still, it also means that we are now part of God's kingdom and have the authority and power to overcome all the works of the enemy.

If we live a righteous life, the Lord becomes the source of our strength.

We need not fear; we can repent and return to God even if we make mistakes.

He forgives us because He loves us.

Psalm 118:6, 8

The Lord is on my side: I will not fear; what can man do unto me? Trusting in the Lord is better than putting confidence in man.

The Lord is always on our side, so we need not fear what others can do to us. Trusting the Lord rather than relying on people is essential.

Whenever we receive an evil report, we should turn to God and ask Him for deliverance.

The Word tells us that we don't have things because we don't ask for them. God wants us to ask Him for whatever we desire, no matter what it is.

The Lord desires to communicate with us, just as He communicated with Adam in the cool of the evening in the Garden of Eden. Therefore, we should feel free to talk with Him and share our thoughts.

Matthew 6:19-34

As per God's teachings, there's no need to worry about anything as He already knows our daily needs. If we worry, it shows our lack of faith in God.

"If God can care for the birds and knows when even one of them falls, how much more will He take care of us, who are created in His image?" A sparrow falls to the ground, and God takes note of it. God knows everything about us, even the number of hairs on our heads.

Making God's kingdom our top priority is crucial, as it promises a life free of fear and worry.

Spending time alone with God can draw us closer to Him and help us trust His provision for all our needs.

Remember, prioritizing God leads to a genuinely fulfilling and purposeful life.

1 John 4:18:

There is no fear in love, but perfect love casts out fear. Fear has to do with punishment; whoever fears has not been perfected in love.

Palm 34:4:

I sought the Lord, and He answered me and delivered me from all my fears,

CHAPTER 10

CULTIVATING COURAGE

Cultivating courage means intentionally taking steps and changing our mindset to confront our fears with strength and determination. Here are some ways to do that:

1. **Face Fears Head-On**

Dealing with fears directly involves confronting what scares us instead of ignoring or running away. This approach empowers us to overcome our fears and move forward with Resilience.

2. **Practice Self-Compassion**

Being kind to yourself means treating yourself with gentleness and understanding, especially when facing fear.

Self-compassion eases the burden of fear, allowing us to navigate challenging times with greater inner strength.

3. **Seek Support**

When feeling scared, seek support from friends, family, or a supportive network. Their encouragement and understanding can give you the strength and reassurance to face your fears and keep moving forward.

4. **Set Realistic Goals**

Breaking down daunting tasks into smaller, manageable pieces makes them easier to handle.

Tackling one step at a time helps you feel less overwhelmed and more in control.

1. **Celebrate progress**

Recognize and cheer for every minor achievement, no matter how small.

Celebrating each step forward builds confidence and motivation, helping you continue towards your goals despite fear.

6. **Challenge Negative Thoughts**

Replace doubtful thoughts with positive statements and trust in yourself.

Focusing on your strengths and capabilities builds self-confidence and Resilience, helping you tackle challenges more optimistically.

7. **Learn from Setbacks**

View mistakes and setbacks as opportunities to learn and become stronger.

Seeing failure as part of learning helps you bounce back with more determination and wisdom.

By changing our thoughts and actions, we can steadily become braver and confront our fears more easily, upgrading our courage bit by bit.

Visualizing Success

Celebrating successes, no matter how small, is essential for cultivating courage.

Acknowledging your progress boosts confidence and reinforces positive behaviours, making it easier to continue facing challenges with determination.

Incorporating these strategies into your life helps cultivate courage and resilience, enabling you to confront your fears, overcome obstacles, and achieve your goals.

Remember, courage is a skill developed with practice and perseverance.

Each step towards facing your fears brings you closer to unlocking your full potential and living a more fulfilling life.

CHAPTER 11

REWRITING THE NARRATIVE

Rewriting the narrative about fear involves fundamentally altering how we perceive and discuss it. Instead of viewing fear as an opposing, paralyzing force, we can reframe it as an essential component of personal growth and an opportunity for empowerment.

This transformative shift helps us approach fear with greater confidence and Resilience.

1. **Acknowledge Fear as a Natural Emotion**

Understanding that fear is a natural and universal human emotion can change how we respond.

Instead of feeling ashamed or weak, we can accept fear as a typical human experience. This acceptance reduces the stigma around fear and encourages open discussions about it.

2. **Reframe Fear as a Learning Opportunity**

Instead of viewing fear solely as a barrier, we can see it as a valuable teacher.

Each fearful situation presents a chance to learn more about us, our limits, and our potential. Embracing fear as a source of insight helps us grow and adapt.

3. **Use Fear to Build Resilience**

Reframing fear as a challenge to overcome rather than an obstacle to avoid can strengthen our resilience.

By confronting concerns directly, we develop coping strategies and Resilience that serve us well in other areas of life.

4. **Shift the Language Around Fear**

The words we use to describe fear can significantly impact our experience.

We can use empowering language. Instead of using negative language that reinforces feelings of helplessness, replace "I am terrified" with "I am facing a challenge." This subtle shift in language can change our mindset and response to fear.

5. **View Fear as a Motivator**

Fear can be a powerful motivator when harnessed correctly. Instead of allowing fear to paralyze us, we can use it as a driving force to prepare, practice, and improve. For instance, fear of failure can motivate us to work harder and diligently towards our goals.

6. **See Fear as a Sign of Growth**

Fear often indicates stepping out of our comfort zones and pushing our boundaries. Recognizing fear as a sign of personal and professional growth can help us embrace it positively.

Each step into the unknown is a step towards expanding our capabilities.

7. **Emphasize Stories of Overcoming Fear**

Sharing and reflecting on stories where fear was faced and overcome can inspire and empower others. These narratives highlight the possibility of triumph despite fear and encourage a culture of bravery and perseverance.

8. **Cultivate a Growth Mindset**

Adopting a growth mindset, where challenges and fears are seen as opportunities to develop new skills, can transform our approach to fear. This mindset fosters a belief in continuous improvement and the potential to overcome obstacles through effort and learning.

We can transform our relationship with it by fundamentally changing how we think and talk about fear.

Viewing fear as a natural part of the human experience and an opportunity for growth allows us to approach it more confidently and with Resilience.

CHAPTER 12

HISTORICAL INDIVIDUALS WHO CONQUERED THEIR FEARS

1. ** Nelson Mandela**

Fear** Oppression and retaliation by the apartheid regime.

Achievement

Nelson Mandela faced the brutal apartheid system in South Africa, which enforced racial segregation and discrimination.

Despite the fear of oppression and severe retaliation, Mandela took a stand against this regime.

He spent 27 years in prison for his activism. Instead of being broken by his long imprisonment, he emerged as a powerful advocate for peace and reconciliation.

After his release, he played a crucial role in dismantling apartheid and fostering a new era of democracy in South Africa.

In 1994, Mandela became the country's first black president, symbolizing hope and Resilience worldwide.

Quote: "I learned that courage was not the absence of fear, but the triumph over it."

Early Life

Mandela was born in 1918 in the rural village of Mvezo, South Africa.

He was the first in his family to receive a formal education.

Activism

He joined the African National Congress (ANC) in 1943. He co-founded the ANC Youth League, advocating for civil disobedience and non-violent resistance.

Imprisonment

Arrested in 1962, Mandela was sentenced to life imprisonment for his anti-apartheid activities.

He spent most of his sentence on Robben Island.

Release and Presidency

Released in 1990 amid growing domestic and international pressure, Mandela led negotiations to end apartheid.

He was elected president in South Africa's first multiracial elections in 1994.

**Legacy*

Mandela's leadership and unwavering commitment to justice have made him a global icon for peace and human rights.

His life and work continue to inspire movements for equality and justice worldwide.

Rosa Parks

Fear of persecution and violence.

Rosa Parks conquered her fear of persecution and violence through a combination of personal determination, supportive networks, and strong moral convictions.

Here's a detailed look at how she managed to overcome her fear:

Personal Determination

Rosa Parks' decision to remain seated was underpinned by a deep personal resolve.

She had long been frustrated with the injustices of segregation and felt a strong moral imperative to act.

Once she decided enough was enough, her commitment to justice and fear of what could happen were overshadowed.

Supportive Networks

1. **NAACP Involvement**

Rosa Parks was an active member of the National Association for the Advancement of Colored People (NAACP).

Her role as the secretary of the Montgomery chapter connected her with like-minded individuals who supported and encouraged her activism.

This network provided emotional and strategic support, reinforcing her courage to stand.

1. **Highlander Folk School**

Rosa Parks had attended training at the Highlander Folk School, which was dedicated to social justice and equality.

This experience gave her the tools and confidence to engage in civil disobedience and to understand that her actions could contribute to broader societal change.

Strong Moral Convictions

DON'T LET FEAR WIN

1. **Religious Faith**

Rosa Parks was deeply influenced by her Christian faith, which taught her the values of dignity, justice, and standing up for what is right.

Her belief in these principles gave her inner strength and a sense of righteousness that helped her overcome fear.

1. **Historical and Familial Legacy**

Rosa Parks drew inspiration from her family, particularly her grandfather, who stood up to white intimidation.

Her family instilled in her a sense of self-respect and the importance of standing up against injustice.

This familial legacy of resistance played a crucial role in shaping her courage.

Key Quote

"I have learned over the years that when one's mind is made up, this diminishes fear." This quote by Rosa Parks captures how she managed her fear.

By making a firm decision to fight against segregation, she was able to channel her fear into determination and action.

Impact and Legacy

Rosa Parks' defiance on December 1, 1955, was not just a spontaneous decision but resulted from years of preparation and contemplation.

Her bravery sparked the Montgomery Bus Boycott, a significant event in the Civil Rights Movement, demonstrating how individual courage can inspire collective action and lead to meaningful social change.

Rosa Parks conquered her fear of persecution and violence through personal resolve, the support of her community, strong moral and religious convictions, and a deep sense of justice and self-respect.

Her ability to overcome fear and take a stand made her a pivotal figure in the fight for civil rights.

Abraham Lincoln
Fear of Failure and National Division
Abraham Lincoln conquered his fear of failure and national division through steadfast determination, a clear moral vision, strategic leadership, and an ability to learn and adapt.

Here's an in-depth look at how he managed these fears:

Personal Determination

Lincoln's rise from humble beginnings to the presidency was marked by numerous personal and political failures.

Despite these setbacks, he developed a resilience that allowed him to face the daunting challenges of his presidency, including the Civil War.

His perseverance and commitment to his goals helped him overcome fear and uncertainty.

Clear Moral Vision

Lincoln's belief in the principles of democracy and the moral imperative to end slavery provided him with a clear sense of purpose.

He viewed the preservation of the Union and the abolition of slavery as intertwined goals that were worth fighting for, regardless of the risks.

This moral clarity helped him maintain his resolve even in the face of tremendous opposition and doubt.

Strategic Leadership

1. **Emancipation Proclamation**

Lincoln's decision to issue the Emancipation Proclamation was a strategic move that redefined the purpose of the Civil War.

By making the abolition of slavery a war aim, he gave the conflict a higher moral purpose, which helped to galvanize public support and keep the Union cause morally and politically focused.

1. **Political Acumen**

Lincoln was adept at navigating the complex political landscape of his time.

He built a coalition of support across different factions within his party. He worked to keep the border states loyal to the Union.

His ability to manage diverse political interests helped him maintain the integrity of the Union.

Learning and Adaptation

Lincoln was not afraid to admit mistakes and learn from them.

He replaced ineffective generals and adjusted his military strategies as the war progressed.

His willingness to listen to differing viewpoints and incorporate new ideas helped him lead the nation through its darkest times.

Inspirational Communication

Lincoln's speeches and writings, such as the Gettysburg Address and his Second Inaugural Address, were instrumental in shaping public opinion and inspiring the nation.

His eloquence and ability to articulate liberty and equality helped to unite people and strengthen their resolve.

Key Quote

"My great concern is not whether you have failed but whether you are content with your failure."

This quote reflects Lincoln's attitude toward failure.

He saw it as a temporary setback rather than a permanent state, focusing instead on perseverance and pursuing a higher goal.

Personal Beliefs and Philosophy

Lincoln's deep belief in democracy and human equality and his study of the Founding Fathers influenced his national vision.

His philosophical grounding gave him the inner strength to endure criticism and setbacks.

Legacy and Impact

Lincoln's leadership ultimately preserved the Union and led to the abolition of slavery. His ability to face and conquer his fears profoundly impacted American history, demonstrating how determination, moral clarity, and strategic leadership can overcome even the most daunting challenges.

Abraham Lincoln left a legacy as one of America's greatest presidents.

He was a testament to his ability to lead the nation through its most challenging period.

CHAPTER 13

CURRENT EXAMPLES OF INDIVIDUALS WHO CONQUERED THEIR FEAR

Malala Yousafzai

Fear of violence and oppression.

Malala Yousafzai overcame her fear of violence and oppression through a combination of personal courage, strong family support, education, and a deep commitment to her cause.

Here's a detailed look at how she managed to conquer her fears:

Personal Courage

Malala demonstrated extraordinary personal bravery from a young age. Growing up in the Swat Valley of Pakistan under Taliban rule, where girls' education was banned, she continued to attend school and publicly advocate for girls' rights.

Her steadfast belief in the importance of education fueled her courage.

Even after being shot by the Taliban in 2012, she remained undeterred in her mission.

Strong Family Support

1. **Father's Influence**: Malala's Father, Ziauddin Yousafzai, significantly influenced her.

An educator and activist, he instilled in Malala a love for learning and a sense of justice.

His encouragement and support played a crucial role in her development as a vocal educational advocate.

2. **Family Resilience**

Malala's family stood by her despite threats and violence.

Their collective resilience and unwavering support gave her a secure foundation to continue activism.

Education and Awareness

1. **Love for Learning**

Malala's passion for education was a powerful motivator.
She believed sincerely in the transformative power of education, not just for herself but for all girls.
This belief gave her the strength to stand up against the Taliban's oppressive regime.

1. **Global Perspective** Exposure to global education campaigns and support from international communities helped Malala understand the broader context of her struggle.

It also provided her with additional platforms to amplify her voice.

Commitment to Her Cause

1. **Advocacy**

After her recovery, Malala continued her advocacy on a global scale.
She co-authored the memoir "I Am Malala," which brought international attention to the issues of girls' education and the impact of violence and oppression.

1. **Malala Fund**

She established the Malala Fund to champion education for girls worldwide, demonstrating her long-term commitment to the cause.
This organization ensures every girl has 12 years of free, safe, and quality education.

Inspirational Communication

Malala's speeches and writings have inspired millions. Her address to the United Nations in 2013, where she said, "One child, one teacher, one book, and one pen can change the world," encapsulated her message of hope and empowerment.

Her ability to articulate her vision has been crucial in rallying support for her cause.

Key Quote

"I tell my story not because it is unique but because it is the story of many girls."

This quote reflects Malala's understanding of her role as a representative of millions of girls who face similar challenges. Her personal story is a powerful tool for highlighting broader issues of violence and oppression.

Moral and Ethical Beliefs

Malala's moral and ethical beliefs, grounded in her upbringing and cultural values, gave her a strong sense of right and wrong. Her conviction that education is a fundamental human right helped her to stay focused and resilient.

Impact and Legacy

Malala's courage and advocacy have had a profound impact on global awareness of girls' education and the challenges posed by violence and oppression.

She became the youngest-ever Nobel Peace Prize laureate in 2014, further solidifying her influence and the importance of her cause.

In summary, Malala Yousafzai overcame her fear of violence and oppression through personal courage, strong family support, a passion for education, and a deep commitment to her advocacy. Her ability to inspire and mobilize people worldwide has made her a powerful symbol of Resilience and the fight for girls' education.

****Elon Musk****

**** Fear of failure and financial ruin.**

Elon Musk conquered his fear of failure and financial ruin through personal resilience, strategic risk-taking, relentless work ethic, and a visionary mindset.

Here's a detailed exploration of how he managed these fears:

Personal Resilience

Musk's journey is marked by numerous challenges and setbacks, yet he has consistently demonstrated an ability to persevere through adversity. His resilience is rooted in his unwavering belief in his vision and mission, whether transitioning the world to sustainable energy or making humanity a multi-planetary species.

Strategic Risk-Taking

1. **All-In Approach**:

Musk is known for his willingness to invest his personal fortune into his ventures. For instance, during the critical periods of SpaceX and Tesla, he risked almost all his wealth to keep the companies afloat.

This all-in approach shows his commitment and belief in the potential of his projects.

1. **Calculating Risks**

While Musk takes significant risks, they are often calculated. He profoundly understands the industries he enters, which allows him to make informed decisions. His confidence in his understanding of technology and markets helps mitigate the fear of failure.

Relentless Work Ethic

Musk's intense work ethic is a crucial factor in overcoming fear. He is known for working extremely long hours, often more than 100 hours a week during critical phases.

This dedication ensures that he is deeply involved in all aspects of his businesses, allowing him to address issues swiftly and effectively.

Visionary Mindset

1. **Long-Term Vision**

Musk's ability to maintain a long-term vision helps him look beyond immediate setbacks. He focuses on the goal rather than short-term failures.

This perspective allows him to stay motivated and reduces the impact of potential failures.

1. **Innovation and Disruption**

Musk thrives on challenging the status quo.

His visionary mindset is driven by a desire to solve big problems and innovate.

This drive for disruption helps him embrace risks as necessary steps toward groundbreaking achievements.

Overcoming Specific Failures

1. **SpaceX**: SpaceX faced several failures in its early years, with multiple rocket launches ending in explosions.

Instead of succumbing to fear, Musk learned from these failures and iterated on the designs.

The successful launch of Falcon 1 in 2008 was a turning point, proving the viability of private space exploration.

2. **Tesla** Tesla has faced numerous challenges, including production delays, financial struggles, and skepticism from the auto industry.

Musk's ability to navigate these challenges, secure funding, and continuously innovate with products like the Model S Model 3 and battery technology has been crucial.

Inspirational Leadership

Musk's leadership style inspires confidence in his team and stakeholders.

His transparency about challenges and failures and his clear articulation of the mission help rally support and keep morale high even during tough times.

Key Quote

"When something is important enough, you do it even if the odds are not in your favour."

This quote by Musk encapsulates his approach to overcoming fear.

He prioritizes the importance of his goals over the fear of failure, driving him to persist despite the risks.

Support System and Mentorship

Musk has also benefited from a strong network of mentors, advisors, and a talented team. Their support and expertise give him additional resources and perspectives to tackle challenges.

Learning from Failures

Musk views failures as learning opportunities.

His iterative approach, especially evident in SpaceX's development process, involves testing, failing, learning, and improving.

This mindset reduces the fear of failure, seeing it as a step towards success.

Impact and Legacy

Musk's ability to conquer his fears has led to transformative impacts in multiple industries, from space exploration and electric vehicles to renewable energy and artificial intelligence.

His legacy is a testament to the power of resilience, vision, and relentless pursuit of ambitious goals.

Elon Musk overcame his fear of failure and financial ruin through personal resilience, strategic risk-taking, relentless work ethic, a visionary mindset, and learning from failures.

His approach to innovation and leadership continues to inspire and drive significant advancements across various fields.

3. **Oprah Winfrey**

** Fear

Oprah Winfrey overcame her fear of poverty and rejection through personal Resilience, a strong sense of self-worth, strategic career moves, and a commitment to personal growth and helping others. Here's a detailed look at how she managed to conquer these fears:

Personal Resilience

1. **Challenging upbringing**: Oprah's early life was marked by poverty, abuse, and instability. Despite these hardships, she developed a strong sense of Resilience. She learned to persevere through adversity, which laid the foundation for her future success.

2. **Education and Self-Empowerment**: Oprah valued education to escape poverty. She excelled in school, earning a scholarship to Tennessee State University. Her dedication to learning helped build her confidence and opened doors to new opportunities.

Strong Sense of Self-Worth

1. **Belief in Potential**: Despite numerous setbacks, Oprah maintained a belief in her potential. She recognized her talents in communication and storytelling from an early age, which motivated her to pursue a career in media.

2. **Positive Self-Image**: Over time, Oprah cultivated a positive self-image and learned to value herself beyond societal standards. This self-acceptance helped her face rejection and criticism with more tremendous fortitude.

Strategic Career Moves

1. **Radio and Television Breakthroughs**: Oprah's career began in radio and local television, where she quickly gained recognition for her natural charisma and interviewing skills. She seized opportunities that showcased her talents, which helped her rise through the ranks.

2. **The Oprah Winfrey Show** Her breakthrough came with "The Oprah Winfrey Show," which she turned into one of the highest-rated talk shows in history.

She built a loyal following and significant influence where she could authentically connect with audiences.

Commitment to Personal Growth

1. **Learning from Experiences** Oprah viewed challenges and failures as learning opportunities. She continually sought to improve herself and her work, which helped her grow both personally and professionally.

2. **Therapy and Self-Reflection* Oprah has sought therapy and deep self-reflection. This commitment to understanding and healing herself helped her overcome past traumas and fears.

Helping Others

1. **Empathy and Connection**: Oprah's empathy and ability to connect with others on a deep level became a hallmark of her success.

She fostered a sense of community and support among her viewers by sharing her struggles and triumphs.

2. **Philanthropy and Advocacy**: Oprah's extensive philanthropic efforts, particularly in education and empowerment, reflect her desire to help others overcome their fears and challenges. Her initiatives, such as the Oprah Winfrey Leadership Academy for Girls in South Africa, profoundly impact many lives.

Key Quote

"You get in life what you have the courage to ask for."

This quote encapsulates Oprah's approach to overcoming fear. By daring to pursue her dreams and ask for what she wanted, she broke through barriers of poverty and rejection.

Building a Support Network

Oprah surrounded herself with supportive mentors, friends, and colleagues.

Their guidance and encouragement gave her the emotional and professional support to navigate her career.

Embracing Failure and Rejection

Oprah did not let failure and rejection define her. Instead, she used them as motivation to improve and prove her worth.

Her early career rejection did not deter her; it propelled her to find the right platform for her talents.

Impact and Legacy

Oprah's journey from poverty and rejection to becoming one of the most influential women in the world is a testament to her resilience, vision, and dedication.

Her legacy is not only in her media empire but also in her lasting impact on culture, philanthropy, and the lives of countless individuals she has inspired and helped.

Oprah Winfrey overcame her fear of poverty and rejection through personal resilience, a strong sense of self-worth, strategic career decisions, a commitment to personal growth, and a dedication to helping others.

Her life story is a powerful example of how determination and self-belief can transform one's circumstances.

These individuals show that overcoming fear is essential for achieving greatness and making a significant impact. Whether fighting for civil rights, leading a nation through crisis, or pioneering in science and technology, their stories inspire us to face our fears with courage and determination.

CHAPTER 14

BIBLICAL FEATS OF CONQUERING FEAR
DAVID AND GOLIATH
1 SAMUEL 17

David's overcoming of his fear of Goliath is a powerful story rooted in faith, preparation, and perspective.

Here are the key factors that contributed to his triumph:

1.   **Faith in God**

David's faith played a crucial role in overcoming his fear.

He had a deep trust in God and believed that God would deliver him from the threat posed by Goliath.

In 1 Samuel 17:37

David says, "The Lord who rescued me from the paw of the lion and the paw of the bear will rescue me from the hand of this Philistine."

His faith gave him confidence that he was not alone and that God was with him.

1.   **Past Experiences**

David drew strength from his past experiences as a shepherd.

He had successfully defended his flock against lions and bears, which boosted his confidence.

His victories were proof of God's protection and support.

These experiences helped him believe that he could also defeat Goliath.

1.   **Proper Perspective**

Unlike the rest of the Israelite army, David did not view Goliath as an insurmountable giant but an opponent who could be defeated.

He viewed Goliath's challenge as defiance against the armies of the living God, which he believed would ensure Goliath's defeat.

David's perspective focused on God's power rather than the size of the giant.

1. **Preparation and Skills**

David's skill with a sling was another critical factor. He had spent years practicing and honing this skill while tending sheep.

This preparation meant that he could use a weapon effectively that others might underestimate.

1. **Courage and Initiative**

David showed immense courage by volunteering to fight Goliath when no one else would. His courage was not born of recklessness but faith, past victories, and confidence in his abilities. David took the initiative to confront the challenge head-on.

1. **Rejecting Conventional Armor**

David chose to fight Goliath with his familiar weapons—a sling and stones—instead of King Saul's armour, which he was not used to. This decision allowed him to leverage his strengths and maintain his agility. David's overcoming of fear involved a combination of his unwavering faith in God, reliance on past experiences of divine deliverance, a unique perspective on the challenge, his preparation and skill with a sling, and his courage to take the initiative.

Together, these elements enabled him to face Goliath confidently and ultimately achieve victory.

MARK 4: 35

DON'T LET FEAR WIN

JESUS CALMS THE STORM – 41

The story of Jesus calming the storm is a well-known event described in the New Testament, found in the Gospels of Matthew, Mark, and Luke.

Here is a summary of the key elements and significance of the story:

The Event

Setting

Location

The Sea of Galilee.

Jesus and his disciples were crossing the Sea of Galilee in a boat after a day of teaching and ministering to the crowds.

The Storm

A furious storm arose suddenly, with waves breaking over the boat, causing it to nearly be swamped.

Disciples' Reaction

The disciples were terrified and feared they would drown.

They woke Jesus, who was sleeping on a cushion in the stern of the boat, and cried out,

"Teacher, don't you care if we drown?" (Mark 4:38).

Jesus' Response

Jesus got up, rebuked the wind, and said to the waves,

"Quiet! Be still!" (Mark 4:39).

The wind died down, and it was completely calm.

Jesus then asked his disciples, "Why are you so afraid? Do you still have no faith?" (Mark 4:40).

1. **Demonstration of Divine Power**

This miracle showcased Jesus' authority over nature, affirming his divine identity.

By calming the storm with a command, Jesus demonstrated his power as the Son of God.

1. **Faith and Fear**

The story highlights the contrast between fear and faith.

The disciples' fear of the storm reflected their lack of faith.

At the same time, Jesus' calm response and question to them emphasized the importance of trusting in him, even in dire circumstances.

1. **Jesus' Care and Presence**

The disciples questioned whether Jesus cared about their plight.

His calming of the storm reassured them of his care and constant presence; even when he seemed "asleep" or not, he immediately responded to their fears.

1. **Lessons for Believers**

The event teaches believers to have faith in Jesus during the storms of life.

It encourages trust in his power to bring peace and deliverance, even when situations seem beyond control.

The story of Jesus calming the storm is a powerful reminder of his divine authority, his care for his followers, and the importance of faith.

It calls believers to trust Jesus' power and presence, even during life's most turbulent challenges.

DON'T LET FEAR WIN

DANIEL IN THE LIONS DEN
DANIEL 6

The story of Daniel in the lions' den is a well-known narrative from the Old Testament, found in the Book of Daniel, chapter 6.

It exemplifies faith, divine protection, and the triumph of righteousness over evil.

The Event

Time and Place

The story takes place during the reign of King Darius of Persia.

Daniel's Position

High Rank

Daniel, an Israelite, had risen to a high position in the kingdom due to his exceptional qualities and God's favour.

He was among the top three administrators overseeing the kingdom's 120 satraps (regional governors).

Jealousy and Plot

Conspirators

Other administrators and satraps became jealous of Daniel and sought to find grounds for charges against him.

Unable to find any corruption or negligence, they targeted his faith.

Decree Against Prayer

They convinced King Darius to issue a decree that for 30 days, no one could pray to any god or human except to the king.

Anyone who disobeyed would be thrown into the lions' den. They knew Daniel's faithfulness to his God would lead him to violate this decree.

Daniel's Faithfulness

Continued Prayer

Despite knowing about the decree, Daniel continued praying three times a day, giving thanks to God, with his windows open toward Jerusalem.

Accusation and Arrest

The conspirators found Daniel praying and reported it to the king.

Although Darius was distressed and sought to save Daniel, he was bound by the irrevocable law of the Medes and Persians.

The Lions' Den

Punishment

Daniel was thrown into the lions' den, and a stone was placed over the mouth of the den, sealed with the king's signet ring and those of his nobles.

Divine Protection

King Darius spent a sleepless night fasting. At dawn, he hurried to the den and called out to Daniel.

Daniel responded, affirming that God had sent an angel to shut the lions' mouths because he was found innocent in God's sight and had not wronged the king.

Deliverance

Rescue and Vindication

Daniel was lifted from the den without injury, demonstrating God's protection.

Punishment of Accusers

The men who had falsely accused Daniel, along with their families, were thrown into the lions' den, where they were immediately overpowered and crushed.

Decree and Praise

King's Decree

King Darius issued a new decree, commanding everyone in his kingdom to fear and reverence the God of Daniel.

He acknowledged God's enduring power, his ability to rescue and save, and his miraculous deliverance of Daniel.

Lessons and Themes:

1. **Faith and Integrity**

Daniel's unwavering faith and integrity, even in the face of deadly consequences, are central themes. His commitment to God was steadfast, regardless of external pressures.

1. **Divine Protection**

The story illustrates God's ability to protect and deliver those who are faithful to him. Daniel's miraculous survival is a testament to God's Intervention.

3.**Justice and Vindication**

The narrative highlights the theme of divine justice. The wicked conspirators faced the fate they had planned for Daniel, emphasizing that evil plots against the righteous ultimately lead to downfall.

God's Sovereignty

4. King Darius's decree and praise of God underscore the recognition of God's supreme power over all earthly authorities.

The story of Daniel in the lions' den is a powerful testament to the virtues of faith, integrity, and divine deliverance.

It encourages believers to remain faithful to God in all circumstances, trusting in his protection and justice.

ELIJAH AND THE PROPHETS OF BAAL
1 KINGS: 18:16-46

The story of Elijah and the prophets of Baal is a dramatic and powerful narrative found in the Old Testament.

This event highlights the conflict between the worship of Yahweh (the God of Israel) and the worship of Baal, a Canaanite deity.

The Event

Time and Place

The story takes place during the reign of King Ahab on Mount Carmel in the northern kingdom of Israel.

Israel was experiencing a severe drought, which the prophet Elijah had predicted because of the nation's idolatry and the evil practices encouraged by King Ahab and his wife, Queen Jezebel, who promoted the worship of Baal.

Confrontation

Challenge Issued

Elijah challenged King Ahab to gather all the people of Israel, including the 450 prophets of Baal and the 400 prophets of Asherah (another Canaanite deity), on Mount Carmel.

Purpose

Elijah aimed to demonstrate God's true power and return the Israelites' hearts to Yahweh.

The Contest

Two Altars

Elijah proposed a contest to determine the true God. Two altars were prepared: one for Baal and one for Yahweh.

Each side would place a bull on their altar but not light the fire. The God who answered by fire would be acknowledged as the true God.

Prophets of Baal

The prophets of Baal prayed from morning until noon, calling on Baal to send fire. They shouted, danced, and even cut themselves, but there was no response.

Elijah's Turn

Preparation

Elijah repaired the torn altar of Yahweh. He used twelve stones to symbolize the twelve tribes of Israel.

He then dug a trench around the altar, arranged the wood, and placed the bull on it.

Soaking with Water

Elijah had the altar and the offering drenched with water three times until the trench was filled with water, igniting the fire seemingly impossible.

Divine Intervention

Prayer and Fire

Elijah prayed to Yahweh, asking Him to demonstrate His sovereignty so the people would know He was God and turn their hearts back to Him.

Immediately, the fire of the Lord fell from heaven and consumed the offering, the wood, the stones, the soil, and even the water in the trench.

People's Response

Witnessing this miracle, the people fell prostrate and declared, "The Lord—he is God! The Lord—he is God!" (1 Kings 18:39).

Aftermath

Prophets of Baal Executed

Elijah commanded the people to seize the prophets of Baal. They were taken to the Kishon Valley and executed.

End of the Drought

Following this, Elijah prayed for rain, and a heavy rainstorm ended the drought, demonstrating God's mercy and power.

1. **Demonstration of God's Power**

The event vividly demonstrates the supremacy and power of Yahweh over false gods. The dramatic contrast between the futile efforts of Baal's prophets and the immediate response from Yahweh underscores His sovereignty.

1. **Elijah's Faith and Courage**

Elijah's actions required immense faith and courage. He stood alone against a large number of prophets and an idolatrous nation, fully trusting in God's power and presence.

1. **Call to Repentance**

The event called the Israelites to repent from idolatry and return to worship the true God. The miraculous fire from heaven was a powerful sign that drew the people back to Yahweh.

1. **Judgment and Mercy**

The story shows God's judgment on false prophets and idol worship (the execution of the prophets of Baal) and His mercy in ending the drought after the people acknowledged Him.

The story of Elijah and the prophets of Baal is a compelling account of faith, divine power, and the call to true worship.

It emphasizes the importance of loyalty to God, the courage to stand against falsehood, and the assurance that God will reveal Himself to those who seek Him earnestly.

THE PARTING OF THE RED SEA
EXODUS 13, 14

The story of the parting of the Red Sea, as recounted in the Book of Exodus, chapters 13 and 14, provides a vivid example of how Moses overcame his fear through faith, obedience to God, and leadership.

Here's a detailed look at how Moses confronted and overcame his fear during this pivotal event:

1. **Faith in God's Promises**

Moses had a deep faith in God's promises and power. Throughout the narrative of the Exodus, Moses consistently relied on God's assurances.

When confronted with the daunting situation at the Red Sea, Moses trusted that God would deliver the Israelites as He had promised.

Trust in God's Plan

Despite the immediate danger posed by the Egyptian army and the seemingly insurmountable obstacle of the sea, Moses believed in God's plan. This faith allowed him to remain calm and composed.

2. **Reassurance from God**

God provided Moses with direct reassurance, which bolstered his confidence and helped him overcome any fear.

God's Instructions

In Exodus 14:15-16, God instructs Moses, "Why do you cry to Me? Tell the children of Israel to go forward. But lift up your rod, stretch your hand over the sea and divide it." These clear instructions gave Moses the direction he needed to act with confidence.

3. **Leadership and Courage**

Moses demonstrated remarkable leadership and courage, qualities that helped him confront his fear and inspire the Israelites.

Encouraging the Israelites

When the Israelites panicked upon seeing the Egyptian army, Moses encouraged them with solid and reassuring words.

In Exodus 14:13-14, he says, "Do not be afraid. Stand still, and see the salvation of the Lord, which He will accomplish for you today.

For the Egyptians whom you see today, you shall see again no more forever. The Lord will fight for you, and you shall hold your peace."

Leading by Example

By taking decisive action, Moses set an example for the Israelites. His calm demeanour and decisive actions stretching his hand over the sea demonstrated his faith and leadership.

4. **Obedience to God's Commands**

Moses' obedience to God's commands, even in the face of fear, was crucial.

Acting on God's Word

Despite the frightening circumstances, Moses did as God instructed. His obedience was a crucial factor in overcoming his fear. He raised his staff and stretched his hand over the sea as commanded, which led to the miraculous parting of the waters.

5. **Witnessing God's Power**

Moses had witnessed God's power through the plagues in Egypt and other miracles, which reinforced his faith and helped him overcome fear.

Previous Miracles

The memory of God's previous acts of deliverance assured Moses that God was with them. These experiences fortified his resolve and courage.

Miracle of the Parting

As the waters parted and the Israelites crossed on dry ground, the visible manifestation of God's power served to eliminate any residual fear Moses might have had.

Witnessing this miracle reaffirmed God's presence and support.

Moses overcame his fear during the parting of the Red Sea through a combination of deep faith in God's promises, direct reassurance from God, his leadership and courage, strict obedience to God's commands, and the reinforcement of witnessing God's power.

His actions facilitated the miraculous escape of the Israelites and solidified his role as a faithful and courageous leader.

This story is a powerful testament to the importance of faith, obedience, and trust in God, especially in the face of seemingly insurmountable challenges.

JOSHUA AND THE BATTLE OF JERICHO
JOSHUA 1:1-9

The story of Joshua and the Battle of Jericho is a remarkable account of faith, obedience, and divine Intervention.

Joshua, who succeeded Moses as the leader of the Israelites, faced significant challenges and fears as he led his people into the Promised Land.

The story of the conquest of Jericho, found in the Book of Joshua, chapters 5 and 6, provides insight into how Joshua overcame his fears and achieved victory.

Here's a detailed look at this narrative:

Context and Preparation

****Leadership Transition****

****Moses' Death****

After Moses' death, God appointed Joshua to lead the Israelites. This transition itself was a significant challenge as Joshua had to step into the large shoes of Moses.

****Divine Commission****

****God's Assurance****

In Joshua 1:1-9, God reassured Joshua with promises of His presence and success. God commanded Joshua to be strong and courageous, emphasizing that He would be with him as He was with Moses.

This divine assurance was critical in helping Joshua overcome his fears.

The Battle Plan

****Encounter with the Commander of the Lord's Army****

****Divine Encounter****

Before the battle, Joshua encountered a divine being described as the Commander of the Lord's army (Joshua 5:13-15).

This encounter reassured Joshua of God's presence and support.

****Unconventional Strategy****

****God's Instructions****

God provided Joshua with a unique battle strategy, unlike conventional warfare tactics. Joshua was to lead the Israelites in a silent march around the city once a day for six days.

On the seventh day, they were to march around the city seven times, with priests blowing trumpets. The people were to shout at the sound of a long blast on the trumpets, and the city walls would collapse (Joshua 6:1-5).

Conquering Fear through Faith and Obedience

1. **Faith in God's Promises**

Joshua's faith was crucial. He believed in the promises God had made to him about the conquest of Canaan.

This faith helped him to trust in the unconventional strategy given by God, even though it might have seemed illogical or impossible.

2. **Obedience to God's Commands**

Joshua's strict obedience to God's instructions was vital. He followed God's plan exactly as described, demonstrating his trust and reliance on God's wisdom and power.

This obedience, even in the face of potential fear and doubt, was crucial in overcoming his fears.

3.Leadership and Encouragement****

Joshua showed strong leadership by communicating God's plan to the Israelites and encouraging them to follow it faithfully. His confidence and unwavering faith inspired the people to trust and follow the divine strategy.

4. **Divine Assurance and Presence**

The repeated assurances from God and the encounter with the Commander of the Lord's army reinforced Joshua's confidence.

Knowing he was not alone and God's presence was with him provided immense courage and strength.

The Victory

Seven Days of Marching

Joshua led the Israelites in marching around Jericho as instructed. They silently marched around the city for six days, with only the priests blowing trumpets.

Seventh Day

On the seventh day, they marched around the city seven times. After the seventh circuit, the priests blew a long blast on the trumpets, and Joshua commanded the people to shout.

Collapse of the Walls

Miraculous Event

At the sound of the trumpets and the shout of the people, the walls of Jericho collapsed, allowing the Israelites to charge straight into the city and capture it (Joshua 6:20).

1. **Divine Intervention**

The victory at Jericho was a clear demonstration of divine Intervention. The miraculous collapse of the city walls showed that the victory was due to God's power, not military might.

2. **Faith and Obedience Rewarded**

Joshua's faith and obedience were rewarded with a spectacular victory. This story emphasizes the importance of trusting and following God's guidance, even when it defies conventional wisdom.

3. **Encouragement for Future Battles**

The conquest of Jericho was a powerful encouragement for Joshua and the Israelites for future battles in the conquest of Canaan.

It reinforced the message that God was with them and would lead them to victory if they remained faithful and obedient.

Joshua overcame his fears through a deep faith in God's promises, unwavering obedience to God's instructions, and strong leadership that inspired confidence in his people.

DON'T LET FEAR WIN

The miraculous victory at Jericho is a testament to the power of faith and obedience, illustrating that seemingly insurmountable obstacles can be overcome with God's guidance and support.

67

PETER WALKING ON WATER
MATTHEW 14: 22-33

The story of Peter walking on water towards Jesus is found in the New Testament, specifically in Matthew 14:22-33.

This narrative highlights Peter's initial faith, his subsequent fear, and the reassurance and support provided by Jesus.

Here's a detailed look at how Peter overcame his fear:

Background

Miracle of Feeding the 5,000

Before walking on water, Jesus had performed the miracle of feeding 5,000 people with five loaves of bread and two fish.

After this, Jesus sent his disciples in a boat to cross the Sea of Galilee while he went up to a mountainside to pray.

The Disciples in the Boat

Stormy Conditions

As the disciples crossed the sea, their boat was buffeted by strong winds and waves, making the journey difficult and frightening.

The Miracle

Jesus Walking on Water

Appearance During the Storm

Early morning, Jesus approached the disciples, walking on the water.

The disciples were terrified, thinking they were seeing a ghost.

Jesus immediately reassured them, saying, "Take courage! It is I. Don't be afraid" (Matthew 14:27).

Peter's Act of Faith

1. Initial Faith and Courage

Peter's Request

Peter, recognizing Jesus, asked, "Lord, if it's you, tell me to come to you on the water" (Matthew 14:28). Jesus replied, "Come."

Stepping Out

Peter displayed remarkable faith and courage by stepping out of the boat and walking towards Jesus on the water.

2. **Moment of Fear and Doubt**

Distraction by the storm

As Peter walked on the water, he noticed the strong wind and became frightened.

His focus shifted from Jesus to the surrounding danger.

Beginning to Sink

Overcome by fear and doubt, Peter began to sink.

He cried, "Lord, save me!" (Matthew 14:30).

Overcoming Fear with Jesus' Help

1. **Jesus' Immediate Response**

Rescue

Jesus immediately reached out his hand and caught Peter.

He said, "You of little faith, why did you doubt?" (Matthew 14:31).

Jesus' swift action prevented Peter from sinking and reassured him of His presence and power.

2. **Restored faith and Calm**

Entering the Boat

The wind died down once Jesus and Peter were back in the boat.

This miracle saved Peter and calmed the storm, providing a physical and symbolic end to the chaos.

1. **Faith and Focus**

Initial Faith

Peter's willingness to leave the boat illustrates his initial faith and trust in Jesus.

Focus on Jesus

When Peter's focus shifted from Jesus to the storm, his fear took over.

This teaches the importance of maintaining focus on Christ amidst life's challenges.

2. **Human Weakness and Divine Strength**

Human Doubt

Peter's fear and subsequent sinking highlight the human tendency to doubt and fear under challenging circumstances.

Divine Rescue

Jesus' immediate rescue of Peter demonstrates His readiness to support and save those who call out to Him, even when their faith wavers.

3. **Encouragement for Believers**
****Overcoming Fear****

Peter's experience encourages believers to trust in Jesus and seek His help when faced with fear and uncertainty. It reassures them that Jesus is always present and ready to assist.

4. **Recognition of Jesus' Divinity**
****Disciples' Response****

After witnessing this miracle, the disciples worshipped Jesus, saying, "Truly you are the Son of God" (Matthew 14:33).

This acknowledgment reinforces the recognition of Jesus' divine authority and power.

Peter conquered his fear of walking on water by initially believing in Jesus and stepping out of the boat.

Although he experienced fear and doubt, his call for help and Jesus' immediate response demonstrated the importance of relying on Jesus in times of fear.

This story is a powerful lesson in faith, the need to focus on Christ, and the assurance of His presence and support in overcoming our fears.

ABRAHAM AND ISAAC
GENESIS 22: 1-19

The story of Abraham and the sacrifice of Isaac is one of the Bible's most profound and challenging narratives.

Found in Genesis 22:1-19, it highlights Abraham's extraordinary faith and obedience to God.

Here's a detailed look at how Abraham overcame his fear and the significance of his actions:

Background

Promise of Isaac

Isaac was the long-awaited son promised by God to Abraham and Sarah.

His birth was a miracle, given Sarah's old age, and he represented the fulfillment of God's promise that Abraham would become the Father of many nations.

God's Command

Testing Abraham

God tested Abraham by commanding him to take his beloved son Isaac to the region of Moriah and sacrifice him as a burnt offering on a mountain that God would show him (Genesis 22:1-2).

Abraham's Response

1. **Immediate Obedience**

Prompt Action

Abraham responded to God's command without hesitation. Early the following day, he set out with Isaac and two servants to the place God had specified (Genesis 22:3).

2. **Faith in God's Promises**

Confidence in God

Despite the terrifying nature of the command, Abraham had deep faith in God.

He believed that God could fulfill His promises even if Isaac were sacrificed.

Hebrews 11:17- 19 explains that Abraham reasoned that God could raise the dead, showing his trust in God's ability to restore Isaac.

3. **Focus on God's Instructions**

****Unwavering Commitment****

Abraham remained focused on God's instructions throughout the journey. He prepared everything needed for the sacrifice, demonstrating his commitment to obey God's command fully (Genesis 22:6-8).

Confronting Fear

1. **Isaac's Question**

****Inquiry****

As they approached the mountain, Isaac asked Abraham about the lamb for the sacrifice. Abraham replied, "God himself will provide the lamb for the burnt offering, my son" (Genesis 22:7-8). This response indicates Abraham's trust in God's provision.

2. **Building the Altar**

****Final Preparations****

Upon reaching the designated place, Abraham built an altar, arranged the wood, bound Isaac, and laid him on the altar (Genesis 22:9).

His actions reflect his determination to follow God's command despite the emotional and psychological turmoil he must have experienced.

Divine Intervention

1. **Angel's Intervention**

****Stop the Sacrifice****

As Abraham raised the knife to slay his son, an angel of the Lord called out to him from heaven, instructing him not to harm Isaac.

The angel affirmed that Abraham's willingness to sacrifice his son proved his fear of God (Genesis 22:10-12).

2. **Provision of the Ram**

****Substitute Offering****

Abraham noticed a ram caught by its horns in a thicket.

He sacrificed the ram instead of his son, recognizing it as God's provision (Genesis 22:13-14).

Aftermath and Significance

1. **God's Blessing**

Renewed Promises

God reaffirmed His promises to Abraham, declaring that because Abraham did not withhold his son, his descendants would be as numerous as the stars in the sky and the sand on the seashore.

Furthermore, through his offspring, all nations on earth would be blessed (Genesis 22:15-18).

2. **Symbolism and Typology**

Foreshadowing Christ

The story often foreshadows God's sacrifice of His Son, Jesus Christ. Just as Abraham was willing to sacrifice his son, God provided His Son as a sacrificial lamb for humanity's sins.

3. **Lessons in Faith and Obedience**

Ultimate Trust

Abraham's actions exemplify ultimate faith and trust in God. His willingness to obey even the most challenging command teaches the importance of trusting God's wisdom and provision.

Fear and Faith

The story highlights how faith can overcome fear. Abraham's fear of losing his son was overshadowed by his greater fear (reverence) of God and trust in His promises.

Abraham overcame his fear of sacrificing Isaac through unwavering faith in God's promises, immediate obedience to God's command, and trust in God's provision.

His actions demonstrated profound trust and reverence for God, a powerful example of faith and obedience.

The divine Intervention and provision of the ram underscore the message that God provides and honours those who trust and obey Him completely.

CHAPTER 15

CONCLUSION AND THE CALL TO ACTION

Fear can be a significant roadblock, casting shadows over our dreams and holding us back. But deep down, we have a strong spirit that can overcome it. This spirit is powered by knowledge, boosted by bravery, and challenged by resilience.

It helps us break free from fear's grip and rediscover our natural sense of happiness and satisfaction.

It's like finding a hidden strength that lets us conquer our fears and confidently chase our dreams.

Understanding acts like a guiding light, leading us through the maze of fear's challenges. It shines a bright beam on the roots and details of our worries, loosening their hold on our minds and giving us a clear view of what's happening.

This knowledge makes us feel stronger and more prepared to face our fears head-on.

It's like turning on a light in a dark room, helping us see our fears for what they really are and empowering us to push past them without getting stuck.

Courage is like our loyal companion, pushing us onward even when fear looms large. It's not about being fearless but summoning the strength to act despite our fears.

With courage leading the way, we boldly step outside our comfort zones, ready to take chances and welcome the unfamiliar with open arms.

Simplified, it's like having a trusted friend who encourages us to face our fears head-on and seize new opportunities, even when we're scared.

Resilience is like a strong fortress protecting us from constant fear attacks. It's the armour that strengthens our inner selves, helping us bounce back from challenges and tough times with unstoppable determination.

Even when fear throws obstacles our way, resilience gives us the power to come out even stronger and more capable, staying true to our goal of pushing through and thriving.

And as we journey through the difficult path beyond fear, it's important to remember that we're not in this alone.

It's like having a team of supporters cheering us on from the sidelines, ready to lend a hand or offer encouragement whenever needed.

When we unite and support, we can lift each other up, offering help and understanding to those who need it. We can stand shoulder to shoulder with friends, offering a hand to lift them up when they stumble and an ear to listen when they need to talk.

In our combined strength, we find comfort and encouragement as we shine a light on the darkness of fear, paving the path for a brighter future full of opportunity and promise.

Let us step boldly into the unknown, armed with understanding, courage, and Resilience as our guiding lights. Though the path ahead may be fraught with challenges and uncertainties, the rewards of living without fear are immeasurable, beckoning us to embrace a life of boundless freedom, fulfillment, and purpose.

In my sincere effort to assist you, the reader, in tackling your fears directly and discovering the vast opportunities that await beyond them, I invite you to join me.

May you discover the bravery to confront uncertainty, the strength to conquer challenges, and the happiness of uncovering your true self as you pursue a life free from the constraints of fear.

It's like extending a hand to help you face your fears and find the unique possibilities waiting for you on the other side.

And in the spiritual realm, where fear often takes root and thrives, let us not forget the ultimate source of our strength and salvation.

The struggle against fear goes beyond just the physical; it's a battle against unseen forces of darkness.

We are fighting against an invisible enemy. As we strive to break free from fear's hold, let's turn to the divine presence of Jesus Christ, inviting Him into our hearts to stand with us and lead us through the turbulent waters of fear.

It's like asking for a powerful ally to help us navigate challenging times and find peace amidst the storm.

Salvation is more than just avoiding eternal punishment—a sacred pledge of being redeemed and revitalized, a complete change of who we are through Jesus Christ's saving grace.

You are getting a fresh start. By believing in Christ's sacrifice and resurrection, we're comforted and reassured as we're lifted out of the darkness of sin and brought into the radiant promise of eternal life. It's like finding hope and a new beginning amid despair.

So, I urge you, dear reader, to answer the call of salvation and accept the grace given to you through Jesus Christ. Only in Him can you find true freedom from fear and the assurance of a life filled with blessings and cherished eternally.

May you journey on this path with steadfast faith and unwavering bravery, knowing that Jesus Christ is right there with you, guiding you every step.

It's like saying, "Take the hand of Jesus and trust in Him to lead you to a life free from fear and full of blessings."

To wrap up this book, I encourage anyone struggling with fear to invite Jesus into their hearts. In fact, you are saying, "Jesus, come live inside me and fight my battles."

Once you welcome Him in, He'll stay with you forever, never leaving you alone or abandoning you.

Let us make it clear to you what salvation means. The Bible clarifies that we have all sinned and need mercy and forgiveness from God."

"Because of our sin, we deserve eternal punishment, but the sinner's prayer is a plea for grace instead of judgment, a request for mercy instead of wrath. Only faith in Jesus' death and resurrection can save us. It is as simple as repeating this prayer.

God, I know I am a sinner. I deserve the consequences of my sin, but I trust in Jesus Christ as my Lord and Savior. I believe His death and resurrection paid the price for my forgiveness. Thank you, Lord, for saving me and forgiving me. Amen!"

Only faith in Jesus' death and resurrection can save us. Jesus assures us he will never leave or forsake us.

If you say this prayer and believe it, you will be saved.

God, I know that I am a sinner. I deserve the consequences of my sin, but I trust in Jesus Christ as my Savior. I believe His death and resurrection paid the price for my forgiveness.

Thank you, Lord, for saving and forgiving me. Amen!

According to John 3:16, we are assured that *God loved the world so much that He gave His only begotten Son, that whosoever believeth in him should not perish but have everlasting life.*

17 For God sent not His Son into the world to condemn the world, but that the world through him might be saved.

Ephesians 2:5-8 tells us that even we were dead in sins, and yet Christ quickened us together with Christ. (By grace, ye are saved.) He raised us up together and made us sit together in heavenly places in Christ Jesus, that in the ages to come, he might show the exceeding riches of His grace in His kindness toward us through Christ Jesus. For by grace are ye saved through faith; and that not of yourselves: it is the gift of God!

May His blessings shower you abundantly as you embark on this sacred journey, and may His love illuminate your path, guiding you toward a life of boundless joy, fulfillment, and purpose. Amen.

Don't miss out!

Visit the website below and you can sign up to receive emails whenever Catharine LJ Parks publishes a new book. There's no charge and no obligation.

https://books2read.com/r/B-A-ABAD-DIPNB

BOOKS 2 READ

Connecting independent readers to independent writers.

Also by Catharine LJ Parks

Obese People
Obesity Strongholds: How to Overcome Them

Standalone
The Ins and Outs of Gastric Bypass
Tips For Successful Dining Out
I am a Keto Kid
Why Remain Morbidly Obese
Ten Fads to Stay Clear of
Don't let Fear Win
Arguing With God

Watch for more at www.catharineljparks.com.

About the Author

Catharine Leona Joy Minter Parks was born in Chatham, Ontario. I am a Keto Kid was published in 2016; Obesity Strongholds and How to Overcome Them was published in May 2016; The Ins and Outs of Gastric Bypass, published July 27, 2017; Tips for Successful Dining Out, and Why Remain Morbidly Obese, was published in 2017.

Read more at www.catharineljparks.com.

www.ingramcontent.com/pod-product-compliance
Lightning Source LLC
Chambersburg PA
CBHW060445160726
47992CB00003B/1086